Save the moments

MAGICAL MOMENTS:

DATE:

50 US States List

DATE of VISIT:

Alabama	AL	....
Alaska	AK	....
Arizona	AZ	....
Arkansas	AR	....
California	CA	....
Colorado	CO	....
Connecticut	CT	....
Delaware	DE	....
Florida	FL	....
Georgia	GA	....
Hawaii	HI	....
Idaho	ID	....
Illinois	IL	....
Indiana	IN	....
Iowa	IA	....
Kansas	KS	....
Kentucky	KY	....
Louisiana	LA	....
Maine	ME	....
Maryland	MD	....
Massachusetts	MA	....
Michigan	MI	....
Minnesota	MN	....
Mississippi	MS	....
Missouri	MO	....

50 US States List

DATE of VISIT:

State	Abbr	
Montana	MT	....
Nebraska	NE	....
Nevada	NV	....
New Hampshire	NH	....
New Jersey	NJ	....
New Mexico	NM	....
New York	NY	....
North Carolina	NC	....
North Dakota	ND	....
Ohio	OH	....
Oklahoma	OK	....
Oregon	OR	....
Pennsylvania	PA	....
Rhode Island	RI	....
South Carolina	SC	....
South Dakota	SD	....
Tennessee	TN	....
Texas	TX	....
Utah	UT	....
Vermont	VT	....
Virginia	VA	....
Washington	WA	....
West Virginia	WV	....
Wisconsin	WI	....
Wyoming	WY	....

ADVENTURE STARTS HERE...

....

ALABAMA

Favorite memories

DATE:

Save the moments

„Veni, Vini, Amavi. We came, we saw, we loved."

ALASKA

Favorite memories

DATE:

Save the moments

„Life is a journey, not a destination."

ARIZONA

Favorite memories

DATE:

Save the moments

„live life with no excuses, travel with no regret." – Oscar Wilde

ARKANSAS

Favorite memories

DATE:

Save the moments

„Good company in a journey makes the way seem shorter." – Izaak Walton

CALIFORNIA

Favorite memories

DATE:

Save the moments

„I never travel without my diary. One should always have something sensational to read on the train." - Oscar Wilde

COLORADO

Favorite memories

DATE:

Save the moments

„There's no way I was born to just pay bills and die".

Save the moments

„Everything you do is based on the choice you make". - Wayne Dyer

DELAWARE

Favorite memories

DATE:

Save the moments

"One's destination is never a place, but a new way of seeing things". - Henry Miller

FLORIDA

Favorite memories

DATE:

Save the moments

"Life is either a daring adventure or nothing at all". - Helen Keller

GEORGIA

Favorite memories

DATE:

Save the moments

„He who would travel happily must travel light". - Antoine de St. Exupery

Save the moments

"Travel and change of place impart new vigor to the mind". - Seneca

IDAHO

Favorite memories

DATE:

Save the moments

"Travel and change of place impart new vigor to the mind". - Seneca

ILLINOIS

Favorite memories

DATE:

Save the moments

"Dare to live the life you've always wanted".

INDIANA

Favorite memories

DATE:

Save the moments

„life is short and the world is wide".

Save the moments

"The journey not the arrival matters". - T.S. Eliot

KANSAS

Favorite memories

DATE:

Save the moments

„Work, Travel, Save, Repeat".

KENTUCKY

Favorite memories

DATE:

Save the moments

„The most beautiful in the world is, of coures, the world itself". - Wallace Stevens

LOUISIANA

Favorite memories

DATE:

Save the moments

„The life you have led doesn't need to be the only life you have". - Anna Quindlen

MAINE

Favorite memories

DATE:

Save the moments

„To Travel is to Live". - Hans Christian Andersen

MARYLAND

Favorite memories

DATE:

Save the moments

„Don't listen to what they say. Go see".

MASSACHUSETTS

Favorite memories

DATE:

Save the moments

"Adventure may hurt you but monotony will kill you".

MICHIGAN

Favorite memories

DATE:

Save the moments

„Better to see something once than hear about it a thousand times".

MINNESOTA

Favorite memories

DATE:

Save the moments

"Traveling - it leaves you speechless, then turns you into a storyteller". - Ibn Battuta

MISSISSIPPI

Favorite memories

DATE:

Save the moments

"Travel makes one modest. You see what a tiny place you occupy in the world". - Gustav Flaubert

MISSOURI

Favorite memories

DATE:

Save the moments

"The gladdest moment in human life is a departure into unknown lands". - Sir Richard Burton

MONTANA

Favorite memories

DATE:

Save the moments

„With the right mindset and spirit, only the sky is the limit".

NEBRASKA

Favorite memories

DATE:

Save the moments

„Live your life by a compass, not a clock". - Stephen Covey

NEVADA

Favorite memories

DATE:

Save the moments

„The goal is to die with memories not dreams".

NEW HAMPSHIRE

Favorite memories

DATE:

Save the moments

„Travel is never a matter of money but of courage". Paolo Coelho

NEW JERSEY

Favorite memories

DATE:

Save the moments

„Once a year, go someplace you've never been before". - Dalai Lama

NEW MEXICO

Favorite memories

DATE:

Save the moments

„I love the feeling of being anonymous in a city I've never been before".

NEW YORK

Favorite memories

DATE:

Save the moments

„You don't have to be rich to travel well". - Eugene Fodor

NORTH CAROLINA

Favorite memories

DATE:

Save the moments

"Then I realized adventures are the best way to learn".

NORTH DAKOTA

Favorite memories

DATE:

Save the moments

"Don't call it a dream... call it a plan".

OHIO

Favorite memories

DATE:

Save the moments

"Wherever you go, go with all your heart!" - Confucius

OKLAHOMA

Favorite memories

DATE:

Save the moments

„Oh the places you'll go." – Dr. Seuss

OREGON

Favorite memories

DATE:

Save the moments

„I'm in love with cities I've never been to and people I've never met."

PENNSYLVANIA

Favorite memories

DATE:

Save the moments

„Take only memories, leave only footprints." - Chief Seattle

RHODE ISLAND

Favorite memories

DATE:

Save the moments

"The biggest adventure you can ever take is to live the life of your dreams."

SOUTH CAROLINA

Favorite memories

DATE:

Save the moments

„You can shake the sand from your shoes, but it will never leave your soul."

SOUTH DAKOTA

Favorite memories

DATE:

Save the moments

„Remember that happiness is a way of travel – not a destination." – Roy M. Goodman

TENNESSEE

Favorite memories

DATE:

Save the moments

„Blessed are the curious for they will have adventures."

Save the moments

"To travel is to discover that everyone is wrong about other countries." - Aldous Huxley

UTAH

Favorite memories

DATE:

Save the moments

"Travel is the only thing you buy that makes you richer."

VERMONT

Favorite memories

DATE:

Save the moments

„Life is a journey. Make the best of it."

VIRGINIA

Favorite memories

DATE:

Save the moments

„A good traveler has no fixed plans and is not intent on arriving." - Lao Tzu

WASHINGTON

Favorite memories

DATE:

Save the moments

„The world is a book and those who do not travel read only one page." - Agustine of Hippo

Save the moments

„Travel makes a wise man better but a fool worse." – Thomas Fuller

WISCONSIN

Favorite memories

DATE:

Save the moments

„All journeys have secret destinations of wich the traveler is unaware." – Martin Buber

WYOMING

Favorite memories

DATE:

Save the moments

„Travel. Because money returns. Time does not."

Save money

NEXT TRIP:

DATE:

NOTES

NOTES

NOTES

NOTES

NOTES

Made in United States
Troutdale, OR
12/30/2023